Copyright, Legal Notice and Disclaimer

Chapters

What Is Coin Collecting?

Anyone who saves one or more coins for any reason is coin collecting. Some collect coins as a hobby while others for immediate or long term financial gain. Some individuals collect to teach their children about math, coins and money. Some people collect because they want to invest now, but plan on passing the collection down to their heirs. Some save a specific coin type or date because it holds sentimental value (gold, silver, error, foreign, ancient, commemorate or proof coins for example). Some collect every major coin made. The list goes on.

Don't let the coin field box you in mentally. There isn't a single person that knows it all and every collector has a different degree of knowledge. In other words, do not let the vast amount of information overwhelm you, everyone started at ground zero, we are here on this earth to help each other.

This book covers all the basics of collecting. It shows you how to get started, what coins to start with, and builds upon this foundation. You will learn about error coins and I will show you the tools needed for this endeavor. This material will appeal to a wide audience, from the beginner collector to the high end investor, who holds large amounts of gold and silver coins and possibly rare coins, yet knows little about the coin world.

A topic that is of prime concern because so many have been taken advantage of, concerns certain coins that have been sold at inflated prices to uneducated collectors and investors – I will show you how not to get cheated. And you will learn why rare coins can make the best investments of any asset class. And we will look at the penny and how children can get into this hobby by starting a penny collection. And in case you are wondering, the lonely penny is not so lonely any more: one recently sold for almost $2,000,000.

Let's define the term "rare coin". What is a rare coin? Is a rare coin one that has considerable value attached to it? The word "rare" means uncommon, distinctive, extreme of its kind. So, a definition of "rare coin" can be a coin that is uncommon in some way and may or may not have value. In other words, some coins are very rare and very uncommon, yet do not have much value. Some are very valuable. I will show you why this is.

Coin collectors, on the other hand, typically think in terms of dollar value, when using the term "rare coin". For example, I have seen very uncommon coins, maybe only a few in existence, have no value and therefore coin collectors would not consider them rare. The problem with the term "rare coin" is that there is no standard definition. Is a coin that is worth $1000 a rare coin or not? If you are interested in buying rare coins, what should you buy? Don't worry it will all become clear to you.

Coins that continually go up in value over time and are hard to find and or buy because they are scarce and when found can only be purchased for much more than their face value, is probably a good definition for "rare coins". As far as investing and this book is concerned, this is the definition we will use. Remember a coin is only worth what somebody is willing to pay for it. I have seen a one of a kind coin worth an estimated $100,000, yet other coins that have had over 50,000 of them minted sell for $50,000 in very good condition. I am going to show you what coins are considered "rare" and why.

Before we get started with the basics of collecting I want to talk about investing because so many of us have coins that have value yet we do not know much about them. And many of us want to know what the income potential of our coins and any coins we might buy, is. Everyone should read the next chapter on investing even if your only goal is to learn how to get started collecting coins because the information will open up a whole new world to you.

Coin Collecting:
What Every Investor Must Know

We are going to explore coins and coin collecting in depth. There are many reasons for this, but as stated, a principle one, and this applies to investors, is to help you develop a strong knowledge of this asset class, so you can make sensible decisions. Certain rare coins and coins made of precious metals like gold and silver, have realized a higher rate of return than any other investment type over time. Yet others do not yield good returns, such as pre-1933 gold coins. And U.S. Mint bullion coins are often purchased at prices that make it hard for the investor to recoup anything, especially over short time periods.

Believe it or not, the long term appreciation for high quality rare coins have achieved returns exceeding those of the major equity indices. Looking back over the past 40 years, rare coins have had a compounded (IRR) rate of return greater than 11%, while the DJIA and S&P500 indices have grown at rates less than 7%. Interestingly, rare coins increased slightly in value between 2006 and 2010, while the equity markets went down. We must balance this information with events of the last few years which have seen the DJIA and S&P500 have extraordinary growth, more than the 7% just mentioned. But the facts over time are clear. Rare coins do very well.

An interesting chart reflecting a long term study shows how well rare coins do over the years. The study compares rare coins to many other asset classes. Silvano DeGenova is one of the world's greatest coin authorities, and his rare coin tracking data is based on real sales. Note how his UNC (uncirculated) returns for 35 years rank above all other investment classes on the following chart:

	Five-Year Holding Period Returns (1970-2005)			
Asset Type	Average	Standard Deviation	Sharpe Ratio	Rank
Silver	5.52%	16.83%	-0.03	14
Gold	8.81%	19.28%	0.14	8
Oil	8.70%	15.79%	0.17	6
Homes	6.12%	2.82%	0.02	11
Land	6.17%	6.35%	0.02	12
MSCI World	7.84%	10.97%	0.16	7
S&P	8.14%	9.29%	0.22	4
DJIA	8.15%	8.72%	0.24	3
T-Bill	6.07%	2.54%	0.00	13
DiGenova AU	7.96%	9.12%	0.21	5
DiGenova UNC	9.50%	10.07%	0.34	1
DiGenova Both	9.07%	9.33%	0.32	2
BU Rolls	7.45%	17.60%	0.08	10
Solomon	6.73%	6.73%	0.10	9
A description of the data is presented in the appendix.				

The fourth line from the bottom (**DiGenova UNC**) shows a return of 9.5%. Compare this to silver, gold, oil and the others. Notice the ranking of from 1 to 14 on the right hand column. The top two rankings are for coins. Again, keep in mind the years for the study, which ended in 2005. The world is different now. The stock market is very robust but coin returns still rank high. You can see why rare coin information is so critical. Let's start at the beginning.

Coin Collecting - Getting Started (Tools)

It's a known fact that coin collectors have a great knowledge of precious metals. The reason for this is simple. Many coins are made of silver and gold, and collectors usually have handled them. This gives them an edge. They are familiar with fake coins and fake gold and fake silver and they know the value of silver and gold coins. If you want to sharpen your precious metal skills you will need to understand more about coins, especially bullion coins. Knowledge is the key. If you know what a rare coin is and how to determine a coins value you will be in a much better position to make investment decisions based upon fact, rather than habit or market trends or suggestions from aggressive sales people.

This is a very good time in the book to take a close look at tools you will need to be successful at coin collecting. I am going to show you exactly what these tools are, why they are needed, what they cost, and how to get them.

The tools are:

- Nitrile gloves
- Two coin books
- A jewelry loupe
- A gram scale
- A magnet
- A digital microscope

Nitrile gloves are used to handle coins because they are very dirty. If you look at a lot of coins in one sitting, they come in handy. You will be amazed at how dirty they get from handling coins.

The above ad from Amazon shows latex free gloves. I also recommend that you get powder free gloves. They come in different sizes, so order accordingly. Always order 100, you will be glad you did. They come in black and blue colors. I like the Dynarex brand. Sometimes Walmart carries them. Harbor Freight also has them at good prices.

Two books that I recommend are: *The Red Book – A Guide Book of United States Coins 2015* by R.S. Yeoman and *Strike It Rich With Pocket Change: Error Coins Bring Big Money* by Ken Potter. The error book is an added bonus to have, but not needed in the beginning. The next two images show them on the Amazon web site.

The spiral bound Red Book works best. Always look for the latest edition.

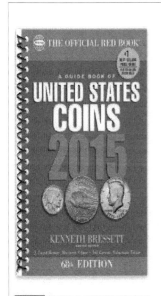

See all 11 images

A Guide Book of United States Coins 2015: The Official Red Book Spiral Spiral-bound

by R. S. Yeoman (Author)

★★★★☆ ▾ 26 customer reviews

#1 Best Seller in Antique & Collectible Reference

▸ See all 3 formats and editions

Hardcover-spiral	Spiral-bound
$16.04	$12.71
8 Used from $11.01	14 Used from $8.66
25 New from $12.04	41 New from $8.56

The Official Red Book - A Guide Book of United States Coins - is 68 years young and going strong. Collectors around the country love the convenience of the spiralbound edition. It opens up and lies flat on a table while you study your coin collection. And of course it includes all the grade-by-grade values, auction records, historical background, detailed specifications, high-resolution photographs, and accurate mintage data that turn a new coin collector into an educated numismatist. How rare are your coins? How much are they worth? The Red Book tells you, covering everything from early colonial copper tokens to hefty Old West silver dollars and dazzling gold coins. You'll find prices for more than 6,000 coins, tokens, medals, sets, and other collectibles. You'll also round out your education in commemoratives, Proof and Mint coins, error coins, Civil War tokens, Confederate coins, private gold, and all the latest National Park quarters, Presidential and Native American dollars, Lincoln cents, and more. Articles on investing, grading coins, and detecting counterfeits will make you a savvy collector, and entertaining essays on the history of American coinage, shipwrecks and hoards, and the modern rare-coin market give you an inside look at "the hobby of kings." These are just some of the features, invaluable Red Book-the world's best-selling coin price guide.

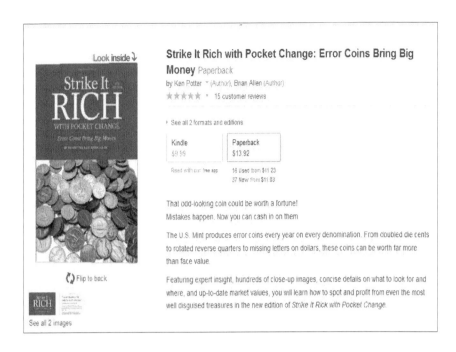

A jewelry loupe is needed to examine coins close up. I buy them on Amazon and prefer those that have a LED light. The loupe shown below works well.

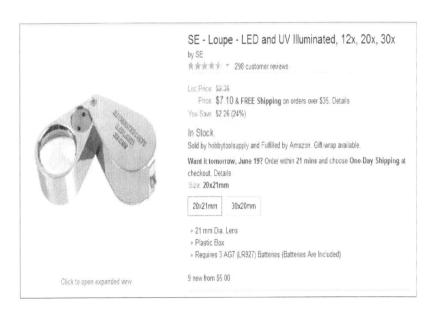

A gram scale is indispensable for weighing coins. These small scales are limited to 8 ounces. Certain coins need to be weighed to determine metal content, authenticity and error types. Make sure the scale you buy weighs in the 100th of a gram as this one does from Amazon. I use the one shown below. It has worked for many years. Shop around on Amazon, prices and products change all the time.

Smart Weigh SWS100 Elite Digital Pocket Scale 100 x 0.01g - Black
by Smart Weigh
★★★★☆ ▾ 27 customer reviews | 3 answered questions
#1 Best Seller in Lab Analytical Balances

List Price: $19.99
     Price: $14.99
        Sale: $9.99 & FREE Shipping on orders over $35. Details
You Save: $10.00 (50%)

In Stock.
Sold by MeasuRite and Fulfilled by Amazon. Gift-wrap available

Want it tomorrow, June 19? Order within 9 mins and choose One-Day Shipping at checkout. Details

* The Elite series is designed with a stainless steel platform and a protective flip cover, this scale is a lightweight and compact size solution for all your portable weighing tasks
* The SWS 100 allows you to weigh a maximum capacity of a hundred grams and readabilities of 0.01g, to guarantee you an accurate and precise weighing session
* Its tactile easy touch buttons, large size digits and stark contrast LCD blue backlight display, makes it easy to read in all light conditions.
* Featuring 4 different weight modes: g / oz / gn / ct for easy weight translations, tare function for net determination and a 60 second auto shut off to preserve battery life
* Use the smart weigh SWS100 scale to measure a versatile range of objects, Such as; Gold, Silver, Coins, Jewelry, Gems and other small knickknacks

Roll over image to zoom in

Here's a real life example of why these small scales are so important. Notice the weight difference, 11.20 grams vs 11.45 grams.

If we did not have the Red Book handy or the internet and had these 2 Kennedy Half Dollars and we were looking at them and noticed their appearance was somewhat different, the gram scale confirms that one weighs more than the other

The 1973 Kennedy on the left has no silver in it – but the 1967 one on the right weighs a little more because it is 40% silver (Can you see the silvery appearance?)

A powerful magnet is used to detect fake coins. This one on Amazon has a handle and is affordable. Remember, even though an item may not stick to the magnet, it can still be fake gold or fake silver or a fake coin. So if someone wants to sell you a gold or silver coin and it sticks to the magnet, you know it is not gold or not silver.

by Master Magnetics

Powerful Handle Magnet with Ergonomic Handle, 4.50" Length, 1" Width, 3.375" Height Including Handle, 100 Pounds Pull, 1 each

★★★★☆ ▾ 27 customer reviews | 3 answered questions

List Price: $9.40
    Price: $5.25 & FREE Shipping on orders over $35. Details
You Save: $4.15 (44%)

In Stock.
Sold by Deerso and Fulfilled by Amazon. Gift-wrap available.

Want it tomorrow, June 19? Order within 0 mins and choose One-Day Shipping at checkout Details

20 new from $4.96

Can you guess how I took this beautiful picture shown below of an 1885 Morgan Silver Dollar? A digital microscope allows you to take great close ups of coins and jewelry. This picture shows its capability. Good quality pictures help when trying to sell an item and when trying to identify a coin. The magnification allows you to see the object close up.

I use this one, displayed above, and it was purchased on Amazon. It plugs into your USB port so make sure it is compatible with your computer ports (USB 2.0 vs 3.0). It comes with software that is amazing. It even takes video. For best results when trying to take pictures of objects that are reflective, move the object to the side slightly so the lights from the microscope are not shinning directly on the object.

Coin Collecting - Clubs and Terminology

Most cities and towns have a coin club. There are a number of reasons to join one, especially if you are new to coins and have children. Here are web sites that have many of the coin clubs around the country listed, along with other useful links:

http://collectingclubs.com/

http://www.coinlink.com/directory/clubs.html

Joining a local coin club is easy and very rewarding. They usually have a low yearly fee, mine is $16. They hold regular meetings, usually once a month and the benefits are enormous:

- They always make educational presentations – great learning resource.
- They are a great way to educate your children. Very few children participate and the members will try to help them – like helping the next generation.
- The members have hundreds of years of coin experience and can help you identify your coins.
- They routinely have auctions where you can buy coins and stamps well below market value.
- Members that you get to know will often have extra coins that they will sell to you at low prices so you can complete your collection.
- Members will buy coins from you.
- Members will have tons of resources – names of reliable dealers e.g. I routinely buy things at my coin club auctions and resell them on eBay.

Terminology is important. Let's define some terms and provide a link to a complete coin dictionary. This link is also a coin forum that is well worth joining, it is free:

http://www.coincommunity.com/dictionary/

Mintmark: A small letter(s) designating where the coin was produced.

C = Charlotte, NC (gold coins only; 1838-1861)

CC = Carson City, NV (1870-1893)

D = Dahlonega, GA (gold coins only; 1838-1861)

D = Denver, CO (1906 to date)

O = New Orleans, LA (1838-1909)

P or No Mintmark = Philadelphia, PA (1793 to date)

S = San Francisco, CA (1854 to date)

W = West Point, NY (1984 to date)

BU: Brilliant Uncirculated refers to the coins condition or grade – it is a coin that is in its original condition or mint state and has original mint luster.

Bullion/Bullion Coin: A coin (American Eagle, e.g.) or other object (bars, ingots, etc…) consisting primarily of a precious metal, e.g. silver, gold, platinum.

Business Strike: A coin minted for general circulation.

Certified: A coin that has been authenticated and graded by one of the major grading services, like: PCGS or NGS.

Circulated: Coins with obvious signs of wear due to being "circulated" in regular commerce.

Clad: Coins made from more than one layer of metal, e.g. quarters since 1965 have a pure copper core, with the outer layers copper-nickel (.750 copper, .250 nickel).

Grade or Grading: A term used to define the coins condition.

Key/Key Date: Refers to the scarcest coins in a series and carries a higher price, e.g. 1909-S VDB Lincoln Cent which is the rarest coin in the Lincoln Penny series.

Luster: The brilliance or shine of a coin and is considered to be one of the main factors in the coins value and grade.

Mint Set: An official set containing one uncirculated coin for each denomination made that year.

MS/Mint State: A term to describe a coin in the condition as it left the mint, uncirculated coins or BU.

NGC: Numismatic Guaranty Corporation is one of the major grading companies.

Numismatics: The study, art or collection of coins, medals, tokens and similar objects.

Numismatist: A person who is knowledgeable in the collecting of coins, medals, tokens and similar objects.

Patina: A term used to describe the lighter shades of toning on a coin.

PCGS: Professional Coin Grading Service is one of the major grading companies.

Proof: A specially produced coin made from highly polished planchets and dies and often struck more than once to accent the design. Proof coins receive the highest quality strike possible and can be distinguished by their sharpness of detail and brilliant, mirror-like surface and sometimes cameo effect.

Proof Set: A complete set of proof coins for each denomination made that year and specially packaged.

Relief: The part of a coin's design that is raised above the surface.

Reverse: The back of the coin or tails.

Rim: The raised outer edge of the coin, that helps protect the design from wear.

Slab: A nickname referring to coins that have been graded by a third party service and placed in a plastic holder.

Strike: The act of impressing the image on to the planchet. The quality of the strike is an important part of the grading process.

Toning: Coloring on the surface of a coin caused by a chemical reaction, such as sulfur from older cardboard books, flips or envelopes. Rainbow-colored toning and original toning is often a desirable characteristic to many collectors.

Type Set: A collection of one coin for each denomination and/or a particular design.

Ask Price: The selling price a dealer offers.

Bid Price: The price a dealer pays for bullion or coins.

Bullion: Precious metals like platinum, gold or silver in the form of bars or other storage shapes. Bullion coins are made of these metals, too.

Collector Coin, Historic Coin, or Numismatic Coin: A coin whose value is based on rarity, demand, condition, and mintage; in fact, it may be worth more than its bullion value.

Melt Value: The basic intrinsic bullion value of a coin if it were melted and sold.

Premium: The amount by which the market value of a gold coin or bar exceeds the actual value of its gold content. The seller can recover part of the premium at resale.

Spot Price: The current price in the physical market for immediate delivery; sometimes called the cash price.

Spread: The difference between the buying price and the selling price.

Troy Ounce: The unit of weight for precious metals. One troy ounce equals 480 grains, 1.09711 ounces, or 31.103 grams.

One of the best ways to learn about coins is by joining a forum. We mentioned one earlier, here are some more:

CoinTalk Forums: https://www.cointalk.com/forums/ These forums are perfect for beginning coin collectors and expert coin collectors. I really love the community here.

Coin Network: http://www.coinnetwork.com/ This site is more than just a coin collecting forum. It is a social network for coin collectors. The Coin Network has a forum section, a blog post section, and a section to create groups.

Susan Headley's Coin Forum: Susan Headley is one of the best coin bloggers. She writes the Susan's Coins Blog at About.com. If you have not read Susan's blog articles, head on over there right now. She is an excellent writer and very passionate about coins. In addition to being a great writer, Susan has a great coin collecting forum.

Collector's Universe Forums: Collector's Universe does not just cater to coin collectors. However, this forum does have an active coin collector community.

Another great forum: www.Coinpeople.com

How To Start Collecting

The best way to learn about coins, even if you have no intention of actually collecting, but want to increase your understanding so your investment strategies can be more fruitful, is to get your hands on some coins and build a small collection. One way to do this is to pick a coin denomination that is easy to work with, costs little, and can be easily found, so you are able to complete a set. Several possibilities come to mind: Lincoln Pennies, Jefferson Nickels and Ancient Coins. Ancient coins are harder to find than pennies and nickels, but are so fascinating that you should consider collecting them.

Of the three listed I suggest Jefferson Nickels. It is very easy to complete a set and this will give you confidence and a sense of accomplishment. You will learn a lot about coins in the process. The Jefferson Nickel came into existence in 1938 to replace the Buffalo Nickel. The most valuable coins are only worth $3 - $15 in good condition, so completing a set is easy and it may require some investing, but not much. Many of the coins can be found in change. Let's look at the type of nickels you may come across:

1938 – 2003 Design (Jefferson front, Monticello back)

2004 - 2005 Design (Westward Journey Series)

2006 – Present (Monticello on reverse again)

The Red Book lists all the dates in the series including some error coins, which are hard to find, and can be expensive, but should be mentioned. We will look at the errors later. A good way to get started is to buy a coin folder that holds the nickels you will be looking for. Several companies make folders: Whitman and H E Harris make folders. Whitman is the cheapest and best for getting started.

The Whitman Folder shown below can be purchased online for as little as $2 used and $3-4 new from Amazon and most major retailers. Three folders are needed for the entire Jefferson Nickel Series.

The Warman folder shown below can be purchased for $4.99 online. It is designed for children and is loaded with educational facts. Amazon has it.

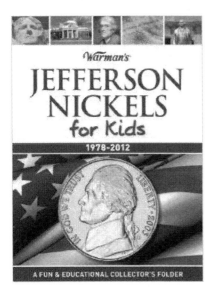

You will notice when you examine the Red Book that there are dates listed that will not be in the coin folders. These are coins that have errors on them, and some coins (not errors) are only minted in special sets and not released into circulation. They show up in change upon occasion, but are not listed in the coin folders. Don't worry about these error and special set dates. Stay focused on the coins listed in the folders. How then does one find the coins to put into the folder?

Besides looking through pocket change, the best way to get your hands on large numbers of nickels is to order a box from the bank. Some banks charge you to do this, some don't. If you have a good working relationship with your bank they will not charge you. Chase, Compass and Citibank are pretty good about this. Each branch is different, so shop around. How then does one order a box of nickels?

Tell your bank to order a box of nickels (not new coins) and they will call you when it comes in, usually three days. You only pay for it when it arrives. A box of nickels holds 50 rolls, $2 each, for a total of $100 and weighs 22 pounds (heavy). This is a dead weight so be careful handling them. They are much heavier than you think.

You have two options when opening these rolls. One is to reuse the roll wrappers by prying one end open carefully with a small flat screw driver. Or, ask your bank for plastic deposit bags. You can dump all the coins into them and mark it with the amount and your bank account number for redeposit (some banks charge for these – they cost the bank about 75 cents each). My bank gives them to me for free.

It is important to know about the metal composition of nickels because at times they are worth a lot more than 5 cents. A standard nickel is 25% nickel and 75% copper. **"War Nickels"** (mid-1942 to 1945) are 56% copper, 35% silver, and 9% manganese. Silver nickels contain 0.05626 troy ounces of silver.

When the price of copper and or nickel rises the actual value of a nickel is more than 5 cents. When this happens people hoard them for resale. All wartime nickels are worth more than 5 cents because of their silver content. The web site coinflation shows them to be worth $.89 each (July 2015).

http://www.coinflation.com/silver_coin_values.html

Any coins found with "S" mint marks should be saved and all silver coins should be saved also (the coin folder has spaces for certain coins, no spaces for newer "S" coins or error coins).

Wartime silver nickels have a mint mark above the dome, see the letter "P" below. It could be a "D" for Denver or an "S" for San Francisco or a "P" for Philadelphia, the cities that minted the coins.

In order to properly identify your Jefferson Nickels that you find it is important to know where the mint marks or letters indicating where the coins were made are located. It can be confusing.

Located from 1938 to 1964 to the right of Monticello, except for "wartime nickels" which have a large mint mark above Monticello shown above (no mint marks used from 1965 to 1967).

From 1968 to 2004, slightly clockwise from the last digit of the date.

In 2005, under "Liberty".

Since 2006, under the date. Philadelphia Mint specimens before 1980 lack a mint mark, except for wartime nickels, which have a P for Philadelphia, if struck there.

When you go through the coin rolls start by looking at the dates and mint marks. As you find coins to fill the slots in the coin folder make sure you have your gloves on. Coins are very dirty. If you find a duplicate coin for a coin already placed in the folder, replace the old one with the new one, if the new one is in better condition, and keep doing this for all the coins. Yes, it is a lot of work, but worth the effort.

Any coins that seem different in some way should be saved, and as stated before, all silver and newer "S" coins should be saved as they have some value. Check the Red Book for coin values and www.coinflation.com for silver and copper-nickel values. When a nickel is worth more than a nickel you should save them.

As you fill the slots you will notice that the empty spaces typically hold the harder to find coins. As you can see in the image below the 1938 D and 1938 S slots are empty. Notice the low mintage figures of 4.1 and 5.4 million.

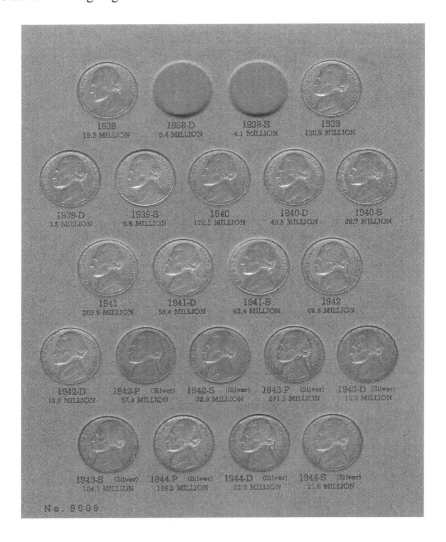

They were minted in low quantities compared to the other coins and therefore are more difficult to find. At some point you might consider purchasing some of these missing coins in order to complete your set. Ebay is a good place to buy coins. We will look at this subject in a future chapter.

Error Coins Can Be Very Valuable

When you start searching for Jefferson Nickels you will immediately notice that the Red Book lists error coins along with the coins you will search for to fill your coin folder. The coin folder has no slots for error coins. Because they have value, I suggest looking for them while searching through rolls of nickels and other coins.

The Red Book mentions eight nickel error types, but if you look at Ken Potters book *Strike It Rick With Pocket Change* he lists thirty error types worth looking for. He states that there are many more, but they are minor in nature. So where does one begin? What does an error coin look like and which ones are worth looking for without spending hours looking at each coin? There is no easy answer, but a good starting point is to look for the eight mentioned in the Red Book and one mentioned on the PCGS web site, the speared bison, for a total of nine.

Let's look at these nine error coins in some detail so you can easily spot them. The Red Book suggests a value for them. The speared bison, not mentioned in the Red Book, is worth $60+. Get out your magnifying loupe – you will need it.

The first error to look for is the 1939 Double Monticello shown below:

You can clearly see the doubling of the letters: O – V – N – S. It is worth $75 or more – value depends upon coin condition.

The 1942D: D/D Horizontal D. The mint mark shows up twice – one over the other. The top "D" is vertical and the bottom "D" is horizontal. It is worth from $75 on up.

1943P: 3 over 2. This one is hard to spot - a faint 2 is present under the 3. It is worth $50 on up.

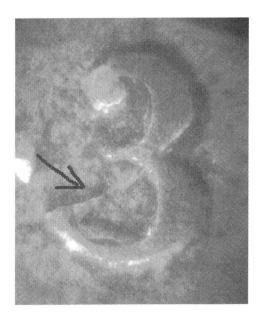

1943P: Double Eye. There is some doubling on the date and letters and the eye – hard coin to spot. It is worth $25 on up.

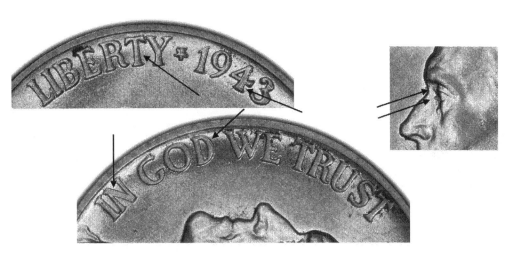

1945P: DDR (Double Die Reverse). You should notice doubling on letters. It is worth $20 and up.

1949D: D over S. It is hard to see this one. It is worth $150 on up.

1954S: S over D. It is worth $26 on up.

1955D: D over S. It is worth $36 on up.

2005D: Speared Bison. It is worth $60 on up.

The easiest way to remember these errors is to make a list of them and keep it handy when looking at the nickels.

- 1939 Double Monticello
- 1942D: D over horizontal D
- 1943D: Double Obverse eye and letters doubled
- 1943: 3 over 2
- 1945D: Double Reverse
- 1949D: D over S
- 1954S: S over D
- 1955D: D over S
- 2005D: Speared Bison

Please keep in mind the fact that error coins can occur at any time on any coin. We looked at nine errors common to the Jefferson Nickel. However, there are some errors that occur when the coin is minted that affect the appearance of the coin, and therefore, can be found at any time on any coin. In other words, the same error may exist on many denominations, pennies, nickels, dimes, etc...

These errors are very noticeable. You can easily see them without any type of magnification. Let's take a few minutes and look at some of them on Jefferson Nickels. Any coin can suffer from these mishaps. The value of these error coins ranges from a few dollars to thousands, depending upon the coin and the error.

This web site gives some values for these errors, also check eBay:

http://coinsite.com/us-error-coin-values/

A rotated reverse or die rotation results in a reverse not being vertical with the front or obverse of the coin - when you flip a coin over the back should be in the same vertical position as the front

The more the coin is rotated the greater the value – just flip each coin over to check for this

A clip error occurs when a new blank coin is punched from a piece of metal that already had a hole in it from previous use.

Off center strikes – coin blank was not placed in collar properly.

Double strikes – coin imprinted more than once.

Lamination error – top layer coming off or not placed on coin properly.

Jefferson Nickel coin blank. Incomplete coin or coin missed its mark, the blank metal onto which a coin is pressed had the rim raised (now called a planchet), but the final imprinting of the coin was never done.

Broadstrike: When a perfectly centered planchet is struck out-of-collar, it expands evenly in all directions. This error can be called a "centered broadstrike". However, since the majority of broadstrikes are centered, hobbyists usually refer to it simply as a broadstrike. If the planchet is not well-centered, but the design remains complete on both faces, the error is called an "uncentered broadstrike".

Dies and Cuds: Extra metal – many variations of this error type. It occurs when the die breaks and extra metal is placed on the coin.

One of the best web sites ever developed on error coins is listed below:
http://www.error-ref.com/index-of-entries.html

This site lists every possible error by name and provides detailed pictures. It is designed for the advanced collector, but worth taking a look at and having as a reference.

Once you look at this site you realize that the error topic in and of itself can become a life time pursuit.

How To Grade Coins

When you start collecting nickels you will notice some are worn out and some look new. As you can imagine, the condition of a coin affects its value. So, to determine value we need a point of reference. The Red Book tells us general values for each coin type based upon a condition that it describes for each coin series.

This image below from the Red Book shows the grades or conditions in relation to the Jefferson Nickel, making this information very valuable for the beginner. It provides a reference point to help determine the condition of the nickels you find.

JEFFERSON (1938 TO DATE)

This nickel was originally designed by Felix Schlag, who won an award of $1,000 in a competition with some 390 artists. His design established the definite public approval of portrait and pictorial themes rather than symbolic devices on our coinage.

Designer Felix Schlag; weight 5 grams; composition (1938–1942, 1946 to date), .750 copper, .250 nickel, (1942–1945), .560 copper, .350 silver, .090 manganese, with net weight .05626 oz. pure silver; diameter 21.2 mm; plain edge; mints: Philadelphia, Denver, San Francisco.

VG-8 Very Good—Second porch pillar from right nearly gone, other three still visible but weak.
F-12 Fine—Jefferson's cheekbone worn flat. Hair lines and eyebrow faint. Second pillar weak, especially at bottom.
VF-20 Very Fine—Second pillar plain and complete on both sides.
EF-40 Extremely Fine—Cheekbone, hair lines, eyebrow slightly worn but well defined. Base of triangle above pillars visible but weak.
AU-50 About Uncirculated—Traces of light wear on only high points of design. Half of mint luster present.
MS-60 Uncirculated—No trace of wear. Light blemishes.
MS-65 Gem Uncirculated—No trace of wear. Barely noticeable blemishes.

1939, Doubled
MONTICELLO and
FIVE CENTS

There is a standard that has been developed to help us decide what the condition or grade is. On a 70-point grading scale coins are assigned a numeric value. It is called the Sheldon Scale. The Sheldon Scale ranges from a grade of Poor (P-1) to Perfect Mint State (MS-70.) Grades are usually assigned at key points on this scale, with the most commonly used points being: (information from about.com)

(P-1) Poor - Barely identifiable; must have date and mintmark, otherwise pretty thrashed.

(FR-2) Fair - Worn almost smooth but lacking the damage Poor coins have.

(G-4) Good - Heavily worn such that inscriptions merge into the rims in places; details are mostly gone.

(VG-8) Very Good - Very worn, but all major design elements are clear, if faint. Little if any central detail.

(F-12) Fine - Very worn, but wear is even and overall design elements stand out boldly. Almost fully-separated rims.

(VF-20) Very Fine - Moderately worn, with some finer details remaining. All letters of LIBERTY, (if present,) should be readable. Full, clean rims.

(EF-40) Extremely Fine - Lightly worn; all devices are clear, major devices bold.

(AU-50) About Uncirculated - Slight traces of wear on high points; may have contact marks and little eye appeal.

(AU-58) Very Choice About Uncirculated - - Slightest hints of wear marks, no major contact marks, almost full luster, and positive eye appeal.

(MS-60) Mint State Basal - Strictly uncirculated but that's all; ugly coin with no luster, obvious contact marks, etc.

(MS-63) Mint State Acceptable - Uncirculated, but with contact marks and nicks, slightly impaired luster, overall basically appealing appearance. Strike is average to weak.

(MS-65) Mint State Choice - Uncirculated with strong luster, very few contact marks, excellent eye appeal. Strike is above average.

(MS-68) Mint State Premium Quality - Uncirculated with perfect luster, no visible contact marks to the naked eye, exceptional eye appeal. Strike is sharp and attractive.

(MS-69) Mint State All-But-Perfect - Uncirculated with perfect luster, sharp, attractive strike, and very exceptional eye appeal. A perfect coin except for microscopic flaws (under 8x magnification) in planchet, strike, or contact marks.

(MS-70) Mint State Perfect - The perfect coin. There are no microscopic flaws visible to 8x, the strike is sharp, perfectly-centered, and on a flawless planchet. Bright, full, original luster and outstanding eye appeal.

A simplified version may be more helpful:

Prefix	Numerical Grade	Description
MS	60–70	Mint State (Uncirculated)
AU	50, 53, 55, 58	About Uncirculated
XF	40, 45	Extremely Fine
VF	20, 25, 30, 35	Very Fine
F	12, 15	Fine
VG	8, 10	Very Good
G	4, 6	Good
AG	3	About Good
FA	2	Fair
PR	1	Poor

Valuable coins, worth $100 or more are often sent to grading companies for certification. Certified coins sell for much more money than the same coin that is not certified, and it lets the seller and buyer know that the coin is not a fake. Buying certified coins assures us that we are getting what we pay for. However, there are certified fakes out there, but not many.

Let's look at some nickels and try to determine their grade or condition.

The Red Book description for a VG-8 Very Good coin shows the 2nd pillar from the right nearly gone, as is the case for the coin below. The other three pillars are visible but worn, so this coin is Very Good or perhaps one grade higher, Fine.

The Red Book states a coin that is AU-50, about uncirculated has traces of light wear on only high points of the design. Half of the mint luster is present. Notice the mint luster.

How To Handle Coins

It is important to know how to handle coins. Coins are dirty, so wearing gloves helps. Handling valuable coins and special coins should be spoken about. Some coins can be damaged just by breathing on them, and some can be damaged by touching them. This results in lowering their value. Valuable coins should never be cleaned by you, only by professionals.

Proof coins, for example, if for some reason need to be taken out of their plastic covers, can be damaged by breathing on them and touching them. Years ago coin holders were not properly made and coins became damaged when stored in them. This problem has been corrected today. The chemical in the holder (usually a card board holder) reacted with the coin, producing a discoloring of the coin or a toning of the coin. Toned coins can have value. The reason I mention this subject is due to the fact that you may come across a very valuable coin and you should only handle it with cotton gloves to maintain its value, no cleaning. Please note: a valuable coin after improper cleaning can be reduced in worth by 90%.

Common coins can be cleaned with soap and water, but no abrasive material or cleanser should be used. Use your fingers to soak the coin in soap and water, do one coin at a time. Rub the coin with your fingers, then rinse the soap and water off with distilled water then place the coin on a towel to dry (don't use your nails).

Because you may come across a toned or sometimes called rainbow toned coin it is important to examine this subject in some detail. Coins react to chemicals around them, either by touch or by exposure through the air. Believe it or not some toned or rainbow toned coins actually are more valuable than plain coins. It depends on the coin and how they look. Never buy a toned coin unless it is certified. Many dishonest sellers bake coins in the oven and produce fake tones.

It is very important that you understand toning. If you clean a toned coin you can take a coin worth maybe $30 - $50 and turn it back into just a quarter, assuming it is a 25 cent piece you just cleaned. Recently PCGS, the coin grading company, tweeted this picture of a Silver Eagle featuring spectacular concentric rainbow toning.

Certified by PCGS – a red coin like this below can sell for hundreds and sometimes thousands of dollars.

Another cleaning method:

Soak the coin in vinegar. If unsightly tarnish, dirt or rust deposits, or other contaminants remain on the coin after a thorough rinse, soak the coin for anywhere from a few seconds to a few minutes. For gold coins, soaking in very hot soapy water works the best. For old pennies, soak the coin in vinegar for at least 24 hours. Silver, copper, and nickel-clad coins can be soaked in distilled water or, to remove tough stains, white vinegar. A 6-minute soak in lemon juice may also be used on silver coins. This will not only protect the coin but it will help give the coin a finish at the end of the cleaning. Always rinse with distilled water and let dry on a clean towel after any cleaning method.

Fake Coins - Buying Safely

Unfortunately it seems that money is more important than ethics, and many places on earth produce vast numbers of fake coins. For example, Lebanon produces fake pre-1933 gold coins. In fact, it has gotten so bad that they even fake certification. They copy the PCGS plastic holder, fake the grading and claim the coin is real when it is not. Fortunately most certified coins are not fake.

Almost every U.S. Mint gold coin has been faked. Many are made in the Middle East. What is so scary about this fake shown below is that it is made of gold and has the same weight as the real coin on the right. Let's look at the reason it is fake.

Counterfeit   Genuine

The coin pictured below is fake – why?

There is moderate softness on both sides but primarily at the digits and letters, which can appear almost cartoonish. There are also a number of raised lines, often seen on fakes, by the denticles, especially on the reverse. A few particularly noticeable raised lines can be seen above the D in UNITED. These are almost never seen on genuine specimens. The denticles are the many little squares around the coin next to the rim. Notice the metal above the D, the extra metal next to the denticle. (Looks like streaks)

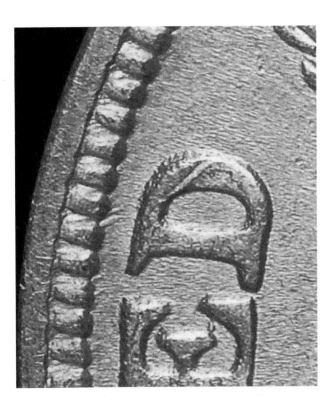

Chinese made fake silver dollars "Morgan" below. The easiest way to spot a fake coin is just by looking at it. Most fakes look perfect, no ware, plastic like, hot off the press.

Photos from Jinghua Shei.

Looks like fake silver coins

Chinese fake coin factory

Fake Indian Head and Large US Cents

Most fake coins will not weigh true. The Red Book tells you the weight of every coin so you can use this as a guide. Many fake coins have incorrect information on them, check the date and mint mark of the coin, and look it up in the Red Book. If the coin in question has a mint mark in the wrong place, the wrong type of mint mark or a date that is not listed in the Red Book, be careful, it may be a fake.

Fake Morgan Silver Dollars and fake older large cent pennies are becoming more common due to the large scale production runs from China and other places. Buying coins online can present challenges, since you cannot test them ahead of time. I will list some steps to help protect yourself. Keep in mind the fact that pictures of coins online from bad dealers may not show the actual coin being sold. Here are some web sites that you can look at to help determine the authenticity of a coin, but this information is usually useful after you buy, not before.

http://coinauctionshelp.com/Counterfeit_Silver_Dollars_Fake_Trade_Dollars_Fak e_Morgan_Dollar.html#.U8PvkEDb4z4

http://www.silver-coins.org/counterfeit_dollars.html

http://meridiancoin.com/contemporary-fake-silver-dollar-guide/

http://www.ngccoin.com/news/viewarticle.aspx?IDArticle=3526&counterfeit-morgan-dollar-fake

If you Google fake coins, fake Morgans, fake silver you will discover more valuable information. You will never end up with a fake coin if you:

• Buy only from a reputable dealer – red flag on eBay are private auctions.
• Buy only slabbed or certified coins (PCGS or NGC).

Picture of a slabbed or certified coin: Coins that have been sent to professional coin grading companies like PCGS, are coins that have been checked for authenticity and enclosed in plastic and their grade or condition is shown on the container. This 50 cent piece minted in 1814 shown below has been graded by PCGS as XF40 or Extra Fine 40. Buying old coins like this one that have been certified, is the only way to protect yourself from fraud. This Judd Plate Coin is worth thousands of dollars.

If you are going to spend over $50 on a coin make sure it is certified or slabbed. Never buy from a dealer that sells slabbed and unslabbed coins – this is a red flag. I see so many dealers online who have a few certified coins and a bunch of coins that have not been graded. I think they do this to convince you they are reputable. Be very careful.

- Many fake coins look like plastic – they look too perfect to be real.
- Many eBay dealers sell fake coins – just look at the pictures.

Another big red flag are dealers who sell coins every week and have large numbers of great coins for sale. It is impossible to have this many good coins unless they inherited them or got their hands on a giant batch of coins from an estate. Even then, I would be very cautious. Probably buying fakes from China.

- Any coin that is worth way more than the asking price is usually fake.

Never buy a coin that you cannot see clearly and in great detail – even a high grade coin may not look so good after you buy it. (I have seen coins on eBay selling for a fraction of their true value – just by looking at them you can tell they are fake).

Another type of fake occurs when an actual coin is altered (the coin is not fake but has been manipulated in some way). A very good article that talks about fake (changed) coins that were sold on eBay is shown below:

http://www.ebay.com/gds/Coin-Fake-Detection-1909-S-VDB-Lincoln-Cent-/10000000015293333/g.html

Let's look at an altered coin:

The highly sought after 1922 penny can be made by removing the "D" from under the date so it appears to be a 1922 coin. Look at the next image.

The "D" is under the date

The highly sought after 1922 penny can be made by removing the "D" from under the date so it appears to be a 1922 coin - This coin was done so skillfully that you cannot see any trace of the "D"

A 1922 "D" coin is worth $20   **A 1922 plain coin is worth $750 - $27,000**

You can see the wisdom of buying only certified coins

When buying online from sites like eBay, it is advisable to make one small purchase from the dealer, and when you get the coin, pay to have it certified. This way you know they are selling genuine merchandise. It is better to pay $30 before shelling out hundreds only to find out you have fakes. You can email me at any time to look at coins in question. This topic will be addressed again in the chapter called: Buying Coins.

Reputable coin companies that certify coins:

www.PCGS.com

www.ngccoin.com

Children and Pennies

Penny collecting is another great way to start learning about coins, and it is a great way to introduce children to this fantastic hobby. What is so sad, is that coin collecting does not appeal to the younger generation because technology offers more pizzazz. Just go to a coin club meeting in any town. There are no young people in attendance. But the good news is if you introduce your children or a friend's or relative's child to penny collecting they will love it. The approach you take is what matters.

The best way for kids to get started is with the Warman's Lincoln Cents For Kids Folder. Amazon has it.

Lincoln Cents for Kids: 1979-2012 Collector's Lincoln Cent Folder (Warman's Kids Coin Folders) Hardcover

by Warman's (Author)

★★★★☆ · 6 customer reviews

Hardcover
from $0.91

28 Used from $0.91
28 New from $0.95
1 Collectible from $15.99

Lincoln Cents for Kids: 1979-2012 collector's Lincoln cent folder

From Lincoln cents to the new National Parks quarters, Warman's coin folders for kids offer everything the young numismatist needs to start on a hobby that could last a lifetime. As you collect, learn why Abraham Lincoln grew his beard, how Thomas Jefferson delivered his addresses to Congress, where the smallest National Park is located and which state features the roadrunner as its state bird. Featuring 75 high-quality die-cut slots and chock-full of fascinating and educational facts, *Lincoln Cents for Kids* is perfect for the young coin collector.

See all 1 images

It is an easy book to fill because it starts in 1979, and it is loaded with fun facts. When working with children they must wear gloves, and very young children should not work with coins because **they are a choking hazard.** I like to order a box of pennies. It is only $25 and contains 2500 coins (caution – it weighs 14 pounds and is dead weight). Lincoln pennies were minted from 1909 – today (see the Red Book).

There is so much you can do with pennies. You can turn the hunt into a game for your kids. They can practice their math skills by calculating the age of pennies they find. See who can find the oldest coin. They will find foreign coins, dimes, shiny new pennies and copper pennies that are worth 2 cents each – see coinflation.com for current rates. You can even find Indian Head pennies, but it takes patience.

Copper pennies were minted from 1909 – 1982 (some 1982 pennies are not copper so you have to weigh them to be sure). A copper penny weighs 3.11 grams. A zinc penny (1982 – present) weighs 2.5 grams. Copper is worth about 2 cents per penny so when children find copper pennies they are doubling their money immediately. This gets them excited. You will find many copper pennies in a box of 2500 coins. This 1974 copper penny shown below weighs 3.08 grams. We know this because of its date.

- The value of a gram scale becomes very apparent now - Some coins can only be verified by weight – fake coins often do not weigh the same as real coins

This 1974 copper penny on the left weighs 3.08 grams – we knew this because of its date – the 2000 zinc penny on the right weighs 2.49 grams

1982 pennies can only be verified by weighing them – some are copper – some are zinc

This zinc penny (2000D) above, only weighs 2.49 grams. Some pennies weigh a little more or less than others, depending upon how worn out they are.

In 1943 the U.S. Mint made pennies out of steel instead of copper. Known as steel war penny or steelie, it had the same design as the copper penny. Due to wartime needs of copper for use in ammunition and other military equipment during World War II, the U.S. Mint researched various ways to limit dependence and meet conservation goals on copper usage. After trying out several substitutes (ranging from other metals to plastics) to replace the then-standard bronze alloy (95 % copper and five % tin and zinc), the one-cent coin was minted in zinc-coated steel. This alloy caused the new coins to be magnetic and 13% lighter. They were struck at all three mints: Philadelphia, Denver, and San Francisco. As with the bronze cents, coins from the latter two sites have respectively "D" and "S" mint marks below the date.

Steel pennies are easy to find and fun to collect. In really good condition (mint) they can easily bring $20 or more. You will find them when looking at penny rolls. Many, however, were destroyed by the government after the war. Notice the gray steel color of the 1943 steel penny on the right compared to the copper penny on the left.

Once children get hooked on coins they will develop a lifelong passion for a hobby that can actually help pay for their education. The Red Book shows the value of pennies, and it shows some error coins as well. My *Penny Treasure* ebook sold on Amazon lists penny coin errors.

A complete Lincoln Penny set in a very high grade can be worth well over $100,000.

The front of the Lincoln Penny has always remained the same since its inception in 1909 – the reverse has had 7 designs listed below

Wheat (1909–1958)

Lincoln Memorial (1959–2008)

Birth and early childhood in Kentucky (Lincoln Bicentennial, 2009)

Formative Years in Indiana (Lincoln Bicentennial, 2009)

Professional life in Illinois (Lincoln Bicentennial, 2009)

Presidency in DC (Lincoln Bicentennial, 2009)

Union shield (2010–*present*)

The world's most expensive penny, a Lincoln cent struck in the wrong metal at the Denver Mint in 1943, sold for a world's record price of $1,700,000 in September 2010:

The Lincoln Penny Series has great appeal to any age group, and it is one of the most sought after coin series in the world of Numismatics. The Whitman Coin Folders can also serve as a starting point for children or for anyone that wants to learn about coins. The next image shows the Whitman Folder Series. Also consider the Harris Folders as well, also made by Whitman. Most large department stores carry these folders. Amazon, as well as other online stores, have them for less money. A good price is $2.99.

Whitman Coin Folder Lincoln Cents 1909-1940

Whitman Coin Folder Lincoln Cents 1941-1974

Whitman Coin Folder Lincoln Cents 1975 to Date

It takes multiple folders to cover the entire Lincoln Penny Series starting in 1909

Special coins, sold only in sets by the US Mint, are not listed in these folders – more expensive folders list all the coins

Penny error coins are well worthy of your time and study, and the Red Book lists some of them. Many are quite valuable, and the major ones can be found when looking through your pennies. Some examples are shown below.

This 1969-S double die penny was graded PCGS MS-64 Red, which is tied with one other specimen for the finest known - It sold at a Heritage auction for $126,500 on January 10, 2008!

Several 1983 "Copper" pennies have been found – at auction they could easily fetch $15000 or more

1983 pennies are normally made of zinc (97.5%) (2.5% copper)

"AM" Separated by Space

"AM" Touching

In 1992 the word "America" on the reverse was supposed to have the letters "AM" far apart instead of almost touching – an example of this error in mint condition sold for over $24,000

Coin Roll Hunting

We briefly mentioned coin rolls with respect to Lincoln Head Pennies and Jefferson Nickels. However, it is important to cover this topic again. I will divide this chapter into two parts, coin roll hunting and buying coin rolls. I could cover the latter, buying coin rolls online, in one word: **DON'T**, but you will then wonder why.

Coin roll hunting refers to the act of opening up coin rolls and looking at the enclosed coins to find a particular coin(s). It could be for the purpose of finding copper pennies, buffalo nickels, silver coins and much more. There is so much mentioned about the topic, especially on YouTube. Most of what you read or see is inaccurate and misleading.

The YouTube videos often mention the frustrations associated with looking at rolled coins. They can't find any silver or they look for certain dates and have little or no success. The problem is very simple. They do not know what they are doing. The only way to be successful at finding silver is by looking through half dollar rolls for 90% and 40% silver coins. And at the same time you should look for half dollar error coins so you have the added bonus of errors along side silver. When you look at half dollars, you will find a lot of 1964 Kennedy Halves because people do not realize that they are 90% silver, and many of them are dirty and hard to spot. Looking for silver with dime and quarter rolls is a waste of time. Looking for quarter errors is not a waste of time. For detailed information on this subject please check out my course: "Learn How Power Sellers Make Millions On eBay" found on www.Udemy.com.

The other topic of interest is buying coin rolls online, especially on eBay. In one word, don't. Almost all the rolls on eBay are fake. They have been manipulated by the seller to appear in such a way that the buyer is tempted to buy or bid because of the end coins that have some value. How is this done?

It is very simple. Just buy a coin crimping machine and some old looking wrappers and put a few Indian Head Pennies at each end and you are in business. Here's a machine on Amazon that can make big money if you were unethical.

Semacon CM-75 Coin Roll Wrapper Crimping Machine (Crimper) w/ 6 Heads
by Semacon
Be the first to review this item

List Price: $775.00
Price: $706.88 + $42.75 shipping
You Save: $68.12 (9%)

In stock.
Usually ships within 2 to 3 days.
Ships from and sold by Sale Stores.

* Safe, you can touch the rotating head while it's spinning and it won't hurt you.
* Requires only a couple of seconds to proficiently seal coin wrappers.
* Includes the following crimping heads: 1¢, 5¢, 10¢, 25¢, 50¢, $1 (SBA/Golden)
* Includes a crimp head storage drawer.

2 new from $700.20

Buying unsearched rolls:

A great article from eBay illustrates my point:

At any given time, eBay has a few hundred auctions for unsearched rolls. The new fad on eBay is bank wrapped rolls showing a key or semi-key date on the end, and the old fad is pointing to their (the seller's) feedback on how many key dates that have been found in the rolls they are selling. Most coins found in bank wrapped rolls are common and well circulated coins. Shot gun wrapped rolls can be opened, searched, then re-crimped as if it came from a bank. The same rolls can be searched and a key date put on the end, then re-crimped as unsearched.

For example, let's say I have a shot gun roll of Lincoln Wheat Cents, and all are common dates. So, I buy a 1909-S key date for $125, (this is the actual book value of the coin in good condition), and I replace the end coin with the 1909-S Lincoln. Also, I know that a 1909-S with the VDB on the back is worth $900, and I also know that you can't see if the 1909-S on the end of the re-crimped roll has a VDB or not. Now I start my auction on eBay with a statement "Unsearched shotgun roll with a 1909-S showing", and a question "Is this a 1909-S VDB?".

I sit back and watch my $125 investment sell for over $255.00 because some buyers wanted to risk the chance to discover a 1909-S VDB. So, they pay $130 more than the roll is worth, and my Paypal account grows over a hundred dollars more. Now I'm thinking, "What if I did this with 10 rolls? I could make well over a thousand dollars in a week!" To top it all off, other eBay sellers see my success and copy my act. Now, it's a huge problem. Don't get into "lottery" wars like this with other bidders. It's never worth it!

Let's look at one of these tempting eBay rolls: Unbelievable, a roll of pennies with an Indian Head at one end probably worth $2 is selling for $42, and the bidding hasn't ended yet.

Look at the seller's feedback below, yet people are still bidding:

⊖	Worthless junk, worn out coins, rolls setup & searched. Waste of good money! unsearched penny roll very old coins lot #31 (#121262431102)	Buyer: i***s (268 ⭐) US $52.01
⊖	Worthless junk, coins all worn, Flying Eagle (reverse)! Rolls set up & searched! unsearched penny roll very old coins lot #32 (#121262433791)	Buyer: i***s (268 ⭐) US $71.09

Rare Coins

The subject of rare coins is of vital interest. We mentioned the term several times before and provided a definition:

Coins that continually go up in value over time and are hard to find and or buy because they are scarce, and when found can only be purchased for much more than their face value, is probably a good definition for "rare coins".

So logic tells us that coins, like most pre-1933 U.S. Mint gold coins, the Double Eagles e.g., are not rare, because they are not scarce. I can prove this to you, and it bears repeating, especially when you consider that thousands continue to buy these coins at prices beyond what they will ever be worth.

- A 1927-D Saint-Gaudens Double Eagle graded NGC MS 66 set a new record for the date when it sold for $1,997,500. With only 12 or 13 examples known, the 1927 $20 gold piece is one of the rarest regular issue United States coins struck 1793 to date.

- Here is a picture of the "Rare Coin"

Here is a listing on eBay for a 1927 Double Eagle just like the one above –
MS66 (same grade) – only difference is that this is a coin minted in
Philadelphia instead of Denver – why is it worth a fraction of the value of
the other coin?

1927 $20 St. Saint Gaudens Double
Eagle Gold PCGS MS66 Coin
Twenty Dollar (*)

FAST 'N FREE - Get it on or before Thu,
Jun. 26

$2,627.00
Buy It Now
Free shipping

There are only a dozen of the other coin in existence – this coin is one of
thousands available

So to claim that Double Eagles in mint states are rare is a completely misleading statement. Advertising pre-1933 Gold Double Eagles as rare coins and using the rare coin index as a point of reference indicating the ROI of around 11% over time is a complete misinterpretation of the facts. Please note: reliable coin dealers and bullion dealers are going with the flow, trying to make a buck. But I think they are somewhat confused about what is rare and what is not rare.

The rare coin index as a term, has many meanings. Its interpretation is a result of what each coin dealer or coin information company or investment journal implies it to be:

For example, the *Wall Street Journal* refers to it this way:

"For the past several years, Coin World has provided a "Classic U.S. Rarities Key-Date Investment Index" for use in the Wall Street Journal's investment scoreboard.

The scoreboard tracks investment groups in the categories of stocks, bonds, mutual funds, bank instruments (bank certificates of deposit and money market accounts), money market funds, precious metals and residential real estate. Coins are listed in the category, "rare coins, top investment grade, in the year-end survey." (Steve Roach)

Here is the index they refer to: (rare coins listed on bottom at 10.30%).

SPECIAL REPORT: YEAR-END REVIEW OF MARKETS & FINANCE
2010 Investment Scoreboard

	TOTAL RETURN ON INVESTMENT		
STOCKS (includes price changes and dividends)	2008	2009	2010
Dow Jones Industrial Average	-31.93%	22.68%	14.06%
Standard & Poor's 500 Stock Index	-37.00	28.46	15.06
Russell 2000	-33.79	27.17	26.85
Dow Jones Wilshire 5000	-37.23	28.57	17.62
BONDS (Barclays Capital Indexes)			
Long-Term Treasury Index	24.03%	-12.92%	9.38%
U.S. Credit Index AA-rated segment	2.74	7.60	7.10
Municipal Bond Index	-2.47	12.91	2.38
Intermediate-Term Treasury Index	11.35	-1.41	5.29
Mortgage-Backed Securities Index	8.52	5.75	5.50
MUTUAL FUNDS			
Lipper Growth Fund Index	-42.24%	35.91%	16.22%
Lipper Growth and Income Fund Index	-37.54	29.10	14.22
Lipper Balanced Fund Index	-26.18	23.35	11.90
Lipper International Fund Index	-43.63	35.30	11.03
Lipper Multi-Cap Value Index	-37.65	26.59	14.54
BANK INSTRUMENTS (Bankrate.com National Index)			
One-Year Certificate of Deposit	2.39%	1.16%	0.65%
30-Month Certificate of Deposit	2.46	1.44	0.99
Money-Market Deposit Account	0.72	0.39	0.21
MONEY MARKET FUND			
iMoneyNet/12-month yield on all taxable funds	2.04%	0.18%	a0.04%
PRECIOUS METALS (S&P Goldman Sachs Commodity Index)			
Platinum	-38.75%	r54.03%	19.35%
Gold	5.83	r22.85	28.73
Silver	-23.84	47.64	81.83
RESIDENTIAL REAL ESTATE			
Office of Federal Housing Enterprise Oversight	-8.16%	-rb4.00%	-3.18%
COLLECTIBLES			
Rare Coins, top investment grade	8.80%	-7.90%	10.30%

r - Revised.
a - Estimated.
b - Through third quarter.
Sources: Thomson Reuters; WSJ Market Data Group; Russell Investments; Coin World (Classic U.S. Rarities Key-Date Investment Index Rare)

In addition to the *Wall Street Journal*, there are many world class coin companies, like PCGS that have their own coin index. PCGS has the PCGS3000. Let's look at it in some detail:

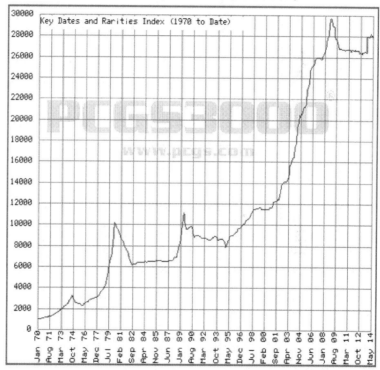

Key Dates and Rarities Index (1970 to date)

[1 year] | [3 years] | [10 years] | [1970 to Date] | [Summary]

The figures in their charts represent an average sale of 3000 rare coins over a period of time. It is based upon prices they monitor and have first hand knowledge of. As you can see in this 44 year chart, rare coin sale prices have increased dramatically. The coins on the lists can be found here: http://www.pcgs.com/prices/PCGS3000.aspx

Let's address the question again, what are rare coins? To begin with, there is no way to invest in the rare coin index because the coins listed are so rare and hard to find that you cannot get your hands on them easily or invest in them as if they are sitting somewhere like a stock or fund. You as a collector, can learn what types of coins are rare, and if money permits, begin buying them in the hopes that they will appreciate about 11% over time, which is what their track record indicates.

- So coin collecting involves learning about Rare Coins and how to acquire them if that is what your objective is

- Let's look at some **very rare** coins – pictures are worth a thousand words:

This 1913 nickel just sold for over $3,000,000

This 1933 double eagle sold for $7,000,000

A coin does not have to be old to be rare – only a few of these test aluminum coins exist

- Coins do not have to be worth millions to be considered rare – some rare coins are worth much less

- Most of the coins listed on the PCGS rare coin list are in high grades but some are not

- eBay auctions - examples of rare coins for sale:

A 1793 VF35 PCGS graded ½ cent

Price is $18,500

This coin is old, rare and in VF condition (not a high grade)

Another example of a rare coin (shown above).

The 1909S VDB Lincoln Penny is a key date in the series and one in this condition is rare. Based upon what you have learned, you should not consider a coin like this that has not been certified by one of the major coin grading companies. Why didn't the seller spend $30 - $40 for certification? I can tell by looking at the coin, based upon an earlier link, that it is real, but I would not take a chance with that much money on the line. The selling price of $910, is far less than the $1500 plus it would have generated had it been graded!

Let's refine the definition of rare coins now that we have looked at some more coins that I consider rare:

Coins that **continually and (dramatically)** go up in value over time and are hard to find or buy because they are scarce, and when found can only be purchased for much more than their face value, and have been **certified by a major grading company**, and most likely are selling for a bare minimum of $300 (most rare coins sell for much more than that), and coins that typically are very old (more than 50 years). Error coins are usually not considered to be rare coins but there are some exceptions.

Major investors in rare coins, such as foreign billionaires, typically buy coins worth millions of dollars knowing that their investment will climb faster than any other asset class. You, however, can enter the rare coin arena with purchases in the $300 - $1000 range (the low end of the rare coin marketplace).

Let's go into the PCGS rare coin index and look at some rare coins so you can get a better feel for ones that the experts consider "rare". I will examine coins on the low dollar end of the index. The next image captures some most people are familiar with, the Lincoln Head Penny:

What I did is capture all the listings for Lincoln Pennies and as you can see there are only 3 dates on the chart: 1909S VDB, 1914D and 1955 DDO

The 1955 is an error coin – the front of the coin is doubled – one of the few error coins on the chart

These are actual coins that were sold and their prices are factored into the index

Let's look at the least expensive coins:

1909-S VDB F12 = $1050
1914-D F12 = $385
1955 F12 = $1500

Note: these dollar amounts are based upon the 2013 Red Book

242612	1909-S VDB	F12	1C	**$1050**	
242630	1909-S VDB	VF30	1C		
242640	1909-S VDB	EF40	1C		
242655	1909-S VDB	AU55	1C		
242863	1909-S VDB	MS63RD	1C		
242864	1909-S VDB	MS64RD	1C		
242865	1909-S VDB	MS65RD	1C		
242866	1909-S VDB	MS66RD	1C		
242867	1909-S VDB	MS67RD	1C		
247112	1914-D	F12	1C	**$385**	
247130	1914-D	VF30	1C		
247140	1914-D	EF40	1C		
247155	1914-D	AU55	1C		
247363	1914-D	MS63RD	1C		
247364	1914-D	MS64RD	1C		
247365	1914-D	MS65RD	1C		
282512	1955	F12	1C	**$1500**	Doubled Die Obverse
282530	1955	VF30	1C		Doubled Die Obverse
282540	1955	EF40	1C		Doubled Die Obverse
282555	1955	AU55	1C		Doubled Die Obverse
282763	1955	MS63RD	1C		Doubled Die Obverse
282764	1955	MS64RD	1C		Doubled Die Obverse
282765	1955	MS65RD	1C		Doubled Die Obverse

You can see from this chart and from these prices that you can enter the rare coin market with small investments like the ones illustrated here. ($385 - $1050 - $1500)

Special Coins

Each year the U.S. Mint makes a limited number of special coins that it sells directly to the public. Examples include: Proof Sets, Mint Sets and Commemoratives. They are usually sold for a premium price because of their unique qualities, and you can sign up to have them sent to you on a regular basis, like an auto ship program. Many who invest in them do so with the expectation of future financial gain, and some just love collecting them.

Proof Sets: Proof refers to the way a coin is made and not a coin's condition. Proof coins are usually sold in sets each year and sold in a protective casing to maintain their beautiful appearance. They are sonically sealed in their case and inspected for quality by U.S. Mint employees wearing gloves (they are not air tight). I have found numerous proof coins in change, apparently someone opened the set to cash in the coins not knowing their value while in the holder. Proofs are commonly known to have mirror like surfaces, but other surface types have been made: Frosted and Matte Proofs are examples.

■ Here's a picture of a proof half dollar I found while coin roll hunting – it pays to look through rolls of coins:

Even though this coin has been worn down from handling it still has its original mirror like proof finish – the reflection of the pen on the coin surface illustrates this point

It is worth very little out of its original case and in this condition, but worth keeping

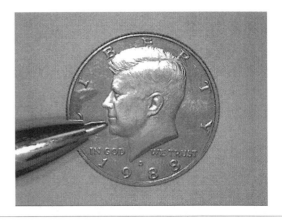

This beautiful 1979S Proof Set has a penny, nickel, dime, quarter, half dollar and dollar coin in it. What is interesting about this set, and this point illustrates how these sets, which are commonly collected for investment purposes, are mistakenly valued, is its current value of $6. It sold for $9.35 in 1979. Had you invested $9 at 1% simple interest for 35 years you would have $12.75 today.

Each year proof sets are minted, and over the years the sets have contained different coin types. The Red Book has a complete list of them. Because of their beauty, they are considered collectible, but the notion that they will increase in value of time is subject to debate. Some do, but most don't. Let's examine this issue in some detail. It has been my experience that owners of proof sets have a misguided sense of their value.

Many proof sets do not increase in value over time. In fact they decrease. Some do appreciate, but at such a slow rate, that they should not be thought of as an investment, just a collectible. The PCGS proof index for the last 10 years bears this out: it shows a minor price increase over a long period of time. There are better ways to invest your money.

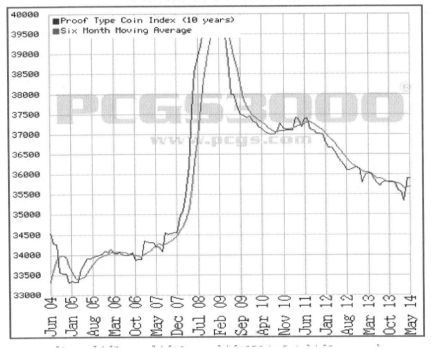

Proof Type Coin Index (10 years)

Mint Sets: Just like proof sets, mint sets are packaged in containers but not sealed like proof sets are. They contain uncirculated, not proof, coins. Most of them are worth less than their original price.

Commemorative coins are authorized by Congress to celebrate and honor historic events, individuals, and places. The coins are legal tender; however, they are not minted for general circulation. Commemorative coins are produced by the United States Mint in limited quantity and are only available for a limited time before minting ceases. Money raised by the sale of these coins helps worthy causes , museums, e.g.. Examples of some commemorative coins recently sold by the U.S. mint:

2009	Abraham Lincoln Commemorative Silver Dollar Program
	Louis Braille Bicentennial Silver Dollar Program
2010	Boy Scouts of America Centennial Silver Dollar
	American Veterans Disabled for Life Silver Dollar
2011	Medal of Honor Commemorative Coin Program
	United States Army Commemorative Coin Program
2012	Star Spangled Banner Commemorative Coin Program
	Infantry Soldier Silver Dollar

Most coins of this type have little future value unless mintage was very small or some other anomaly takes place. In the modern era, the two most valuable coins are the 1997 Jackie Robinson $5 Gold Coin and the 2000 $10 Library of Congress bi-metallic gold and platinum coin. The Jackie Robinson coin, commemorating Major League Baseball's first black player, achieved just six percent of its authorized minting. The 5,174 pieces that were issued are now worth an estimated $3,500 to $6,000. Just 7,261 of the Library of Congress coins were minted, now fetching about $3,750 to $5,200.

This 50th anniversary coin to celebrate the 1964 Civil Rights Act may not have future value because of the large quantity being minted, but for those of us who were alive then it has special meaning. See the image below:

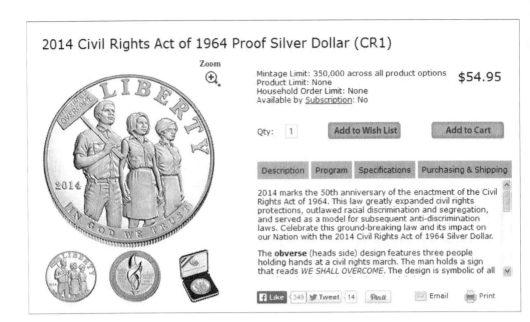

2014 Civil Rights Act of 1964 Proof Silver Dollar (CR1)

Zoom

Mintage Limit: 350,000 across all product options
Product Limit: None
Household Order Limit: None
Available by Subscription: No

$54.95

Qty: 1   Add to Wish List   Add to Cart

Description | Program | Specifications | Purchasing & Shipping

2014 marks the 50th anniversary of the enactment of the Civil Rights Act of 1964. This law greatly expanded civil rights protections, outlawed racial discrimination and segregation, and served as a model for subsequent anti-discrimination laws. Celebrate this ground-breaking law and its impact on our Nation with the 2014 Civil Rights Act of 1964 Silver Dollar.

The **obverse** (heads side) design features three people holding hands at a civil rights march. The man holds a sign that reads WE SHALL OVERCOME. The design is symbolic of all

Like 349 Tweet 14 Pinit   Email   Print

The U.S. Mint also makes medals that can be purchased. Some examples below:

George W. Bush 3" Bronze Medal (146)

Price: $39.95   Qty. 1

Add to Wish List   Add to Cart

George W. Bush 1 5/16" Bronze Medal (846)

Price: $6.95   Qty. 1

Add to Wish List   Add to Cart

William J. Clinton (2ndTerm) Bronze Medal 3" (145)

Price: $39.95   Qty. 1

Add to Wish List   Add to Cart

William J. Clinton (2nd Term) Bronze Medal 1-5/16" (845)

Price: $6.95   Qty. 1

Add to Wish List   Add to Cart

Commemorative coins and some of the other coins mentioned are a great place to start if you are new to the hobby of coin collecting. Each type has a unique design. Participating allows collectors to invest in precious metals (not all of these coins are made of precious metals) that double as legal tender. Purchasing these coins as soon as they are released may turn out to be a valuable investment as time reveals the coin's eventual worth. However, most over time do not appreciate much.

Buying Coins

We briefly spoke about buying coins in a previous chapter. I wanted to make some more key points to help you buy coins. Buying coins from reputable dealers helps prevent fraud.

Years ago buying coins was a very simple process: either you went to your local coin shop or you bought from a coin magazine or journal. Now you still have a few coin shops, and there are some coin magazines, but most buyers look for sources online. Many come to mind: eBay, Amazon, small coin dealer web sites, major coin auction sites, craigslist, local online classified sites, forums that sell coins and smaller coin auction sites. There are also some newer sites like Ubid, Ebid, Onlineauction and Delcampe. Most of the coins on these newer sites are either junk or fake.

While eBay has become the de facto standard for coin purchases, I do want to talk about other options. My experience with smaller coin auction sites suggests that you can often find good deals on them, but you do not have the forms of protection that eBay gives buyers such as buyer protection, easy pay system using PayPal, the ability to check feedback and search history of the seller, a good quality photo system so you can see the coin detail, a wide selection, easy and effective search methods and more.

However, with this in mind, you can often find a coin you really want and need for your collection on these smaller sites and sometimes on local classified.

Some sites to consider: www.vcoins.com. This site has some nice coins and dealers have to abide by a code of ethics. U.S., Ancient and Foreign coins are listed. You can sign up for their free newsletter.

Amazon has beefed up its coin listings with its new coin collectibles section: http://www.amazon.com/Collectible-Coins/b?ie=UTF8&node=9003130011

It has a search tab and many category selections.

There are two coin auction companies/coin dealers that also need to be mentioned. These are the two most important coin companies in the world with respect to auctioning valuable coins. They also sell coins, typically expensive coins.

www.ha.com   Heritage Auctions is the world's largest coin dealer and coin auction house and probably one of the best. You can buy single coins and some at modest prices. This is a good place to find rare coins, and it is one of the best bets for selling your valuable coins.

http://www.stacksbowers.com/   Stacks Bowers is another large and well respected coin dealer-auction house. You can buy coins on this site.

http://www.coincommunity.com/   Coin community is a great forum and source for finding coins.

Your local coin club is also a great way to buy good quality coins from people you can trust. I have seen some good ads on Craigslist for coins, so keep that in mind.

It is important to spend a few minutes talking about a concept that you must come to understand. The term "Key Dates" is a term that is often used to describe the key or best coins in a series.

A "Key Date" is a coin or coins from a set of coins or series of coins, such as the Lincoln Head Penny series, starting in 1909 that is considered very hard to get and much more expensive than the other coins in the set. There are no pre-defined definitions for each set. Just look at the Red Book and look at a series and you will very quickly see the "Key Dates". The coins with the big prices are usually the "Key Dates".

When you start collecting you will soon notice that your coin folder fills up with the easy to find coins, but the key dates remain elusive. Many collectors can only fill in the Key Dates by buying them or trading for them. I mention this subject because of a technique that I have used and recommend to you. I call it "buying down".

I am not suggesting that you buy all your coins, but this technique should be part of your thought process in case you want to try it. It works like this:

I cannot tell you how many times I have seen The Lincoln Penny series, for example, selling on eBay in very good condition but missing the key dates. I consider the key dates for the Lincoln Series to be: 1909S, 1909S VDB, 1914D, 1922, 1931S. Sets like these (missing the key dates) in very good condition often sell for well under $200. Old pennies can be hard to find in change so if you want to jump start your collection, consider this approach. Buy the coins and then try to slowly find (buy) the key dates.

The downside to this is that you cannot see the coins close up (sometimes sellers have good pictures of each coin, but usually not). I trust sellers who sell sets like these.

Sets like these show up on eBay quite often.

Let's look at eBay again and mention some basic rules that will help protect you when purchasing:

• Coins priced over $50 should be **slabbed or graded**. Enclosed in plastic and graded by **PCGS or NGC.**

• Never buy coins unless you see very clear pictures of the front and back.

• Only buy from a seller that has a very good track record – read their feedback carefully.

• Look for bargains by searching for auctions that end at odd hours – such as in late night hours or on days when people are not online much – week days during the mornings, for example.

• Coins that look brand new and are old and priced very low are usually fake.

• Dealers selling coins via private auction are hiding something

• Dealers who sell coins that are graded and also coins that are not graded are hiding something – be very careful. They grade a few coins to make it seem they are legit and then sell fake coins along with the real ones.

• Dealers who always seem to have great coins for sale very week are selling fake coins. Trust me, no one has great coins to sell over and over again unless they bought out a giant estate with thousands of coins in it.

• Always buy only one coin from a dealer or seller and then have it certified. It it passes certification then you know the seller is on the up and up. Only buy from sellers that communicate well with you. I always write to my sellers and ask questions about the coins: How long have you had them? Where did you get them?

I do this not so much because I need these questions answered, but because I can tell by their answers if I want to do business with them – do they answer quickly and provide detailed information. I have seen eBay sellers who answer you in riddles – they try to be vague and often make no sense – they are hiding something.

If you find a coin that you want to purchase, I suggest you save it or put it in your watch list and only bid at the last minute. I never place a bid until the very end. If I am not available when the auction ends, I use a sniping tool to place the bid for me, and I decide how much I am willing to pay. The tool places the bid for you at the last minute, and bids up according to your limit. This way you spend the least amount of money possible and no more than your limit. What is a fair price to pay for a coin? Look it up in the Red Book and use their price as a guide. And you can check eBay for similar coins to see what they are selling for. Don't worry if you do not win a bid. The same coin will show up again.

There are a few good auction tools out there:

https://www.ezsniper.com/index.php3 Ezsniper works well and you get three free auction bids and pay 1% after that for any auction that you win.

There are free sniping tools as well that have good reviews:

https://www.jbidwatcher.com/

http://www.gixen.com/index.php

Another tool that can help analyze a seller's feedback for you is:

www.auctionshadow.com

Conclusion and Summary

Coin collecting is a hobby and or an investment opportunity that anyone can start with very little money and some basic knowledge. The problem that I have noticed over the years, is that collectors who just have the beginning skills start buying coins, anticipating a very large future return. When the time comes to sell their coins, shock sets in, when they are told their coins have no extra value and many times that they are fakes.

I have a good friend who lives in California and he showed me some of the coins he purchased on eBay for $50 - $300. I told him the coins were complete fakes and that coins with those dates on them and in such good condition were worth $5000 on up not $50 - $300. With just a little knowledge and research he could have spared himself this fraud. In fact, when I told him they were fake I never heard from him again. Perhaps he was embarrassed.

I have done my best to provide information in this book which will force you to proceed with great caution before buying. And when you plan on spending at least $50 or more for a coin make sure it is certified or slabbed.

Coin collecting is so much fun and so rewarding that I have written numerous books on the subject. Please take advantage of them on Amazon Kindle. Please let me know if I can be of assistance to you. I will look at any coin that you are considering to purchase, and I do this for free:

storm@ctaz.com

May your days be filled with of joy and happiness – remember those in need.

Made in the USA
Columbia, SC
18 May 2020